Items should be returned on or before the date shown below. Items not already requested by other borrowers may be renewed in person, in writing or by telephone. To renew, please quote the number on the barcode label. To renew online a PIN is required. This can be requested at your local library.
Renew online @ www.dublincitypubliclibraries.ie
Fines charged for overdue items will include postage incurred in recovery.
Damage to or loss of items will be charged to the borrower.

918 . 2

Leabharlanna Poiblí Chathair Bhaile Átha Cliath
Dublin City Public Libraries

Comhairle Cathrach
Bhaile Átha Cliath
Dublin City Council

Due Date	Due Date	Due Date

info buzz

Argentina

Izzi Howell

W

FRANKLIN WATTS

LONDON•SYDNEY

Franklin Watts
First published in Great Britain in 2018 by The Watts Publishing Group
Copyright © The Watts Publishing Group, 2018

Produced for Franklin Watts by
White-Thomson Publishing Ltd
www.wtpub.co.uk

ISBN: 978 1 4451 5958 4
10 9 8 7 6 5 4 3 2 1

Credits
Series Editor: Izzi Howell
Series Designer: Rocket Design (East Anglia) Ltd
Designer: Clare Nicholas
Literacy Consultant: Kate Ruttle

The publisher would like to thank the following for permission to reproduce their pictures: Alamy: David R. Frazier Photolibrary, Inc 10; Getty: elxeneize 6t, Karol Kozlowski 7b, karlagarciav 8t, saiko3p 9, cristianl 12, holgs 17, imigra 18, GerhardSaueracker 19t; Shutterstock: sunsinger cover and 14, Det-anan title page and 11, Alfonso de Tomas 4l, railway fx 4r, pavalena 5, saiko3p 6b and 7t, A Jellema 8b, Aneta_Gu 13t, Christian Vinces 13b, Mai Groves 15t, CP DC Press 15b, T photography 16, Ekaterina Pokrovsky 19b, Ververidis Vasilis 20, giulio Napolitano 21.

Every attempt has been made to clear copyright. Should there be any inadvertent omission please apply to the publisher for rectification.

Printed in China

Franklin Watts
An imprint of
Hachette Children's Group
Part of The Watts Publishing Group
Carmelite House
50 Victoria Embankment
London EC4Y 0DZ

An Hachette UK Company
www.hachette.co.uk
www.franklinwatts.co.uk

MIX
Paper from
responsible sources
FSC® C104740

All words in **bold** appear in the glossary on page 23.

Contents

Where is Argentina?

Argentina is a **country** in **South America**.

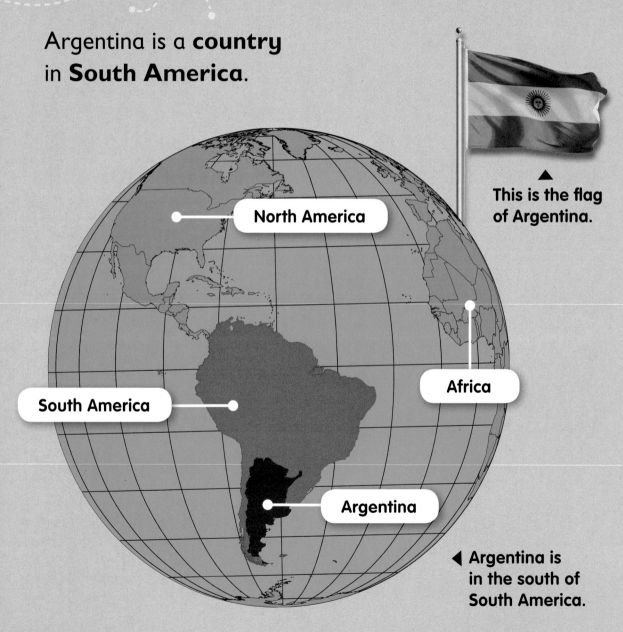

North America

South America

Africa

Argentina

This is the flag of Argentina.

◀ Argentina is in the south of South America.

BOLIVIA

BRAZIL

Argentina is next to other countries, such as Brazil and Chile. ▶

CHILE

PARAGUAY

Iguazu Falls

• Salta

ARGENTINA

PACIFIC OCEAN

• Mendoza

URUGUAY

BUENOS AIRES

ATLANTIC OCEAN

FALKLAND ISLANDS (UK)

Ushuaia •

Argentina is a large country. Its **coast** is on the **Atlantic Ocean**.

Which countries are next to Argentina?

Cities

Buenos Aires is the **capital city** of Argentina. It is the biggest city in the country.

◄ There are colourful buildings in Buenos Aires.

Some of Argentina's **laws** are made in this building in Buenos Aires. ▼

There are cities across Argentina. Ushuaia is at the bottom tip of the country. Salta is in the north.

The weather in Ushuaia is cold. ▶

◀ People can take a **cable car** to the top of a hill in Salta.

Countryside

The centre of Argentina is covered in **grassland** and farms. There aren't many trees.

◀ Argentinian farmers who ride horses are called gauchos.

Farmers let their sheep eat grass on the grasslands. ▼

8

In the south of Argentina, there are mountains with ice and snow. There are huge blocks of ice called **glaciers** between some of the mountains.

▼ Ice melts into water at the end of a glacier.

Interesting places

This huge sculpture is in Buenos Aires.
It is built to look like a flower.

**The sculpture's petals can
move to make the flower
open and close.** ▼

▲ Visitors can get close to the waterfalls in boats.

The Iguazu Falls are a group of waterfalls. They are on the **border** between Argentina and Brazil.

How would you feel if you were near a waterfall in a boat?

11

Food and drink

People in Argentina often eat meat. They cook different types of meat on a barbecue.

◀ Some kinds of meat cook on the barbecue for several hours.

Which Argentinian food or drink on these pages would you like to try?

Mate is an Argentinian drink.
It is made with plant leaves
and hot water,
like tea.

Mate is made in
a special cup.
People drink it
with a metal straw. ▶

◀ Argentinians like
to eat alfajores –
biscuits filled
with caramel.

Sport

Pato is a **traditional** Argentinian sport. Players ride on horseback. They have to throw a ball into a hoop.

A pato ball has six handles.

The Argentinian rugby team (in blue) play against other teams from around the world, such as Australia.

Many people in Argentina like to play football and rugby. They also watch football and rugby matches.

Argentinian football fans cheered for their team at the 2014 World Cup. ▼

Do you have a favourite sports team? Which team is it and why do you support them?

Festivals

In March, people in the city of Mendoza **celebrate** the grape **harvest**. There are parades in the streets.

These boys are playing music in a parade to celebrate the grape harvest.
▼

16

In August, there is a tango festival in Buenos Aires. The tango is a traditional dance from Argentina. It is a dance for two people.

▲ During the tango festival, dancers perform in the street.

Wildlife

Animals such as guanacos and foxes live in the grasslands and mountains of Argentina.

▼ **Guanacos eat grass and other plants.**

Which birds live in your country?

◀ Flamingos live in lakes in Argentina. They eat tiny animals and plants that live in the water.

Different birds live in lakes and on the coast of Argentina.

Penguins come to the south coast of Argentina. They lay their eggs and look after their chicks there. ▼

People

Lionel Messi is a football player from Argentina. He is the captain of the Argentinian football team.

Messi also plays football for Barcelona Football Club in Spain. ▼

Pope Francis is the **leader** of the **Catholic Church**. He was born in Argentina.

◀ Pope Francis wears special robes and a necklace with a crucifix on it.

crucifix

Quiz

Test how much you remember.

1 Name a country that is next to Argentina.

2 What is the capital of Argentina?

3 What is a gaucho?

4 What is mate made from?

5 When is the grape harvest festival?

6 Who is Lionel Messi?

Check your answers on page 24.

Glossary

Atlantic Ocean – the ocean between the east of North and South America and the west of Europe and Africa

border – the line that divides two countries

cable car – a vehicle that is pulled on thick wires

capital city – the city where a country's government work

Catholic Church – the part of the Christian religion that has the Pope as its leader

celebrate – to do something fun on a special day

coast – the land by the sea

country – an area of land that has its own government

glacier – a large block of ice that moves very slowly between mountains

grassland – a large area of land covered in grass

harvest – when crops are ready to be picked

laws – the rules of a country that everyone has to follow

leader – the person in charge of something

South America – a continent that includes countries such as Brazil, Argentina and Venezuela

traditional – describes something that has been done in the same way for many years

Index

Answers:

1: Brazil, Chile, Uruguay, Paraguay, Bolivia; 2: Buenos Aires; 3: An Argentinian farmer who rides a horse; 4: Plant leaves and hot water; 5: March; 6: An Argentinian footballer

Teaching notes:

Children who are reading Book band Purple or above should be able to enjoy this book with some independence. Other children will need more support.

Before you share the book:

* Show children different world maps and globes. Ensure they understand that blue represents sea and other colours show the land.
* Help them to orientate their understanding of the globe by pointing out where Argentina is in relation to North America, Africa and Antarctica.
* Talk about what they already know about South America and Argentina.

While you share the book:

* Help children to read some of the more unfamiliar words.
* Talk about the questions. Encourage children to make links between their own experiences and the information in the book.
* Compare the information about Argentina with where you live. What is the same? What is different?

After you have shared the book:

* Talk about the weather in Argentina. What do children know about the weather in Brazil (to the north) and Antarctica (to the south)? How would this help them to predict weather in Argentina?
* Challenge children to find out more about gauchos and their lifestyle.
* Work through the free activity sheets at www.hachetteschools.co.uk

Countries

Argentina

978 1 4451 5958 4

Where is Argentina?
Cities
Countryside
Interesting places
Food and drink
Sport
Festivals
Wildlife
People

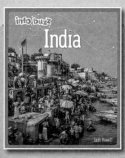

India

978 1 4451 5960 7

Where is India?
Cities
Countryside
Weather
Interesting places
Food
Sport
Festivals
Wildlife

Japan

978 1 4451 5956 0

Where is Japan?
Cities
Countryside
Interesting places
Food
Sport
Festivals
Wildlife
Art

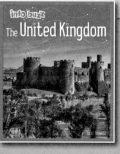

The United Kingdom

978 1 4451 5954 6

Where is the UK?
Capital cities
Countryside
Interesting places
Food and drink
Sport
Festivals
Wildlife
People

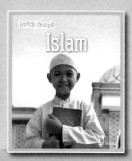

Islam

Religion

Christianity
978 1 4451 5962 1
Hinduism
978 1 4451 5964 5
Islam
978 1 4451 5968 3
Judaism
978 1 4451 5966 9

Queen Elizabeth II

History

Neil Armstrong
978 1 4451 5948 5
Queen Elizabeth II
978 1 4451 5886 0
Queen Victoria
978 1 4451 5950 8
Tim Berners-Lee
978 1 4451 5952 2

Paramedics

People who help us

Doctors
978 1 4451 6493 9
Firefighters
978 1 4451 6489 2
Paramedics
978 1 4451 6495 3
Police Officers
978 1 4451 6491 5

FRANKLIN WATTS